Supreme Diabetes Diet Cookbook

SUPREME DIABETES DIET COOKBOOK

Delicious And Easy To Cook Healthy Recipes For Every Home

THOMAS A. WHITE

Supreme Diabetes Diet Cookbook

All rights reserved. No part of this publication may be reproduced, distributed, or transmitted in any form or by any means, including photocopying, recording, or other electronic or mechanical methods, without the prior written permission of the publisher, except in the case of brief quotations embodied in critical reviews and certain other noncommercial uses permitted by copyright law.

Copyright © THOMAS A. WHITE 2024

Supreme Diabetes Diet Cookbook

TABLE OF CONTENTS

INTRODUCTION
BREAKFAST RECIPES
    Overnight Oats
    Greek yogurt parfait
    Breakfast smoothies
    Egg and vegetable scramble
    Veggie burger and sweet potato fries
    Roasted salmon and vegetable skewers
    Chicken and brown rice bowl
    Turkey and cheese pinwheels
    Black bean and corn salad
    Chicken and avocado salad
    Greek yogurt and fruit parfait
    Roasted vegetable and quinoa bowls
LUNCHTIME RECIPES
    Breakfast quesadilla
    Egg and cheese muffins
    Lunchtime Sandwich
    Grilled chicken salad
    Lunch burrito
    Salmon with quinoa and steamed broccoli
DINNER RECIPES
    Turkey chili
    Shrimp and zucchini noodles
    Baked chicken and sweet potato
    Eggplant Parmesan

Supreme Diabetes Diet Cookbook

- Black bean and quinoa salad
- Beef and broccoli stir-fry
- Vegetable and bean soup
- Grilled turkey and vegetable skewers
- Frozen Yogurt Bark

CONCLUSION

Supreme Diabetes Diet Cookbook

INTRODUCTION

Welcome to the 'Supreme Diabetes Diet Cookbook: Delectable and Simple Healthy Recipes for Every House'. You understand how difficult it may be to keep up a healthy, balanced diet if you or a loved one has diabetes. With so many variables to take into account, such as blood sugar levels, portion control, and the need to avoid particular components, navigating the world of food options can feel overwhelming. But having diabetes doesn't mean you have to stop appreciating delicious meals. This cookbook is actually intended to demonstrate to you that eating a diabetes-friendly diet can be satisfying, flavorful, and varied in addition to being healthful.

Your recipe book, the *Supreme Diabetes Diet Cookbook*, will help you prepare healthy, tasty meals that meet the dietary requirements of people with diabetes. We've carefully chosen a selection of meals that are high in nutrients and simple to make, giving your body everything it needs to flourish. Regardless of your level of experience in the kitchen, these recipes are meant to be simple, approachable, and most importantly, pleasurable to prepare. This book contains a vast array of recipes, ranging from filling breakfasts that will carry you through the day to satiating lunches and dinners, as well as decadent desserts that won't raise your blood sugar. Every dish has been meticulously created with a focus on balance: the ideal ratio of fiber-rich carbohydrates, healthy fats, and proteins to maintain stable blood glucose levels. With every recipe, we also include comprehensive nutritional information so you can plan your diet with knowledge. This cookbook, however, is about adopting a healthy lifestyle that your whole family can enjoy, it's not just about controlling diabetes.

These recipes are for everyone who wants to eat healthily and feel wonderful, not only people with diabetes. All people benefit from following the guidelines of a diabetes-friendly diet, which include consuming whole foods, cutting back on refined sugars, and managing portion sizes. This implies that you may cook these meals for your whole family and be confident that they will receive the nutrition they require. In addition, this book offers helpful pointers and recommendations on managing portion sizes, streamlining meal planning, and adapting your favorite recipes to suit diabetics by substituting components. We'll offer you advice on how to assemble the ideal pantry and create shrewd food selections that complement your wellness objectives.

Supreme Diabetes Diet Cookbook

The goal of this cookbook is to provide you the tools you need to take charge of your health in a way that feels fulfilling and long-lasting. We acknowledge that managing diabetes presents everyday challenges, but we also think that a full and active life can be had with the appropriate resources and attitude. This book's recipes and tips are intended to assist you in achieving this goal by incorporating healthy eating into your daily routine and making it fun. Prepare to explore a whole new world of delectable, diabetes-friendly food as you turn the pages of the *Supreme Diabetes Diet Cookbook*. Every recipe is a step toward greater health, so you can feel secure whether you're cooking for yourself or sharing it with loved ones. Together, let's set out on this adventure to change our eating habits, one delicious and nourishing meal at a time.

BREAKFAST RECIPES

Supreme Diabetes Diet Cookbook

Overnight Oats

Overnight oats are yet another option for persons with diabetes who are looking for a breakfast that is both nutritious and easy. To prepare oats that are let to sit overnight, you will want the following ingredients:

Ingredients
- ½ cup of old-fashioned rolled oats
- ½ cup of unsweetened almond milk
- 1 tablespoon of chia seeds
- ½ cup diced fruit
- 1 tablespoon of chopped nuts or seeds

Directions

Supreme Diabetes Diet Cookbook

Place the oats, almond milk, chia seeds, and diced fruit in a jar or other container that has a lid that can be secured securely. In order to mix, stir. Cover the jar and place it in the refrigerator for at least six to eight hours, or overnight, whichever comes first. The oats should be stirred in the morning, and chopped nuts or seeds should be sprinkled on top. Depending on your preference, you may either serve the oats cold or heat them in the microwave.

Greek yogurt parfait

Individuals who have diabetes may find that a parfait made with Greek yogurt is an alternative for breakfast that is not only simple but also quick and easy to prepare. The following components are required in order to successfully prepare the parfait:

Ingredients
- 1 cup of plain Greek yogurt
- ½ cup of mixed berries
- 1 tablespoon of chopped nuts

Supreme Diabetes Diet Cookbook

Directions

Arrange the Greek yogurt and the mixed berries in a layered fashion in a bowl or container. Garnish the berries with the chopped nuts and sprinkle them on top. Continue to layer the ingredients until the bowl or jar is completely full, including a layer of nuts at the very top. Immediately serve the parfait, or cover it and place it in the refrigerator until you are ready to have it.

Breakfast smoothies

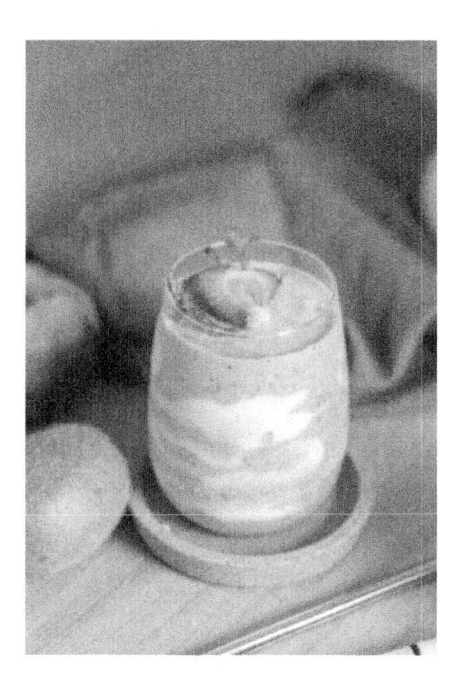

Patients diagnosed with diabetes have the option of consuming a breakfast smoothie, which is both simple and healthful. Listed below are the components that you will need in order to prepare the smoothie:

Ingredients
- 1 cup of unsweetened almond milk
- 1 scoop of vanilla protein powder
- ½ cup of frozen berries

- 1 handful of baby spinach

Directions

Put all of the ingredients into your blender and process them so that they are completely smooth. The smoothie should be poured into a glass, and it should be served right away.

Egg and vegetable scramble

For individuals who have diabetes, another straightforward and wholesome breakfast option is a scrambled egg and veggie dish in the morning. In order to prepare the scramble, you will require the following components with you:

Ingredients
- 1 tablespoon of oil
- 1 cup of diced vegetables
- 4 eggs, beaten
- Salt and pepper
- Whole grain toast or a small portion of cooked potatoes for serving

Directions
Bring the oil to a simmer in a large saucepan set over medium-high power. After adding the diced

veggies, continue to boil them while tossing them occasionally until they are soft and have a light brown color. Turn the heat down to a medium setting. Once the eggs have been beaten, add them to the pan. Eggs should be scrambled until they are completely cooked through. To customize the flavor of the scramble, season it with pepper and salt. If you so wish, you may serve the scramble with toast made with whole grains or a tiny quantity of potatoes that have been cooked.

Supreme Diabetes Diet Cookbook

Veggie burger and sweet potato fries

In order to facilitate the preparation of a veggie burger and sweet potato fries for individuals who have type 2 diabetes, the following ingredients will be required:

Ingredients
- 1 cup of uncooked quinoa
- ½ cup of canned black beans, rinsed and drained
- ½ cup of grated carrots
- ¼ cup of chopped fresh parsley
- ¼ cup of chopped red onion
- 2 cloves of garlic, minced
- 1 teaspoon of ground cumin
- ½ teaspoon of salt
- ¼ teaspoon of black pepper
- 1 large sweet potato, cut into ¼ inch fries
- 1 tablespoon of olive oil
- ¼ teaspoon of paprika
- ¼ teaspoon of garlic powder

Directions
Prepare the quinoa in accordance with the directions provided on the package. After the quinoa has finished cooking, stir it with a fork to fluff

it, and then set it aside to cool. Combine the quinoa that has been cooked, the black beans, the grated carrots, the parsley, the red onion, the garlic, the cumin, the salt, and the pepper in a large mixing bowl. In order to blend, thoroughly mix. The mixture should be formed into four burger patties. Set your oven to 425 degrees Fahrenheit and butter a baking sheet with a light coating. Place the sweet potato fries in a large mixing basin and add the olive oil, paprika, and garlic powder. Toss to combine. On the baking sheet that has been prepared, arrange the french fries in a single layer.When the fries are ready, bake them for fifteen to twenty minutes, or until they are golden brown and crispy. In the meantime, bring a big skillet to a temperature of medium heat. The vegetable burger patties should be cooked in the skillet for five to six minutes on each side, or until they are completely heated through and have a coating that is somewhat crispy on the outside. When it is time to serve, divide the sweet potato fries among the plates that will be used, and then place the veggie burger patties on top of them. Take pleasure in the hot sweet potato fries and veggie burger you ordered.

Roasted salmon and vegetable skewers

In order to properly prepare skewers of roasted salmon and vegetables for individuals who have diabetes, you will require the following ingredients:

Ingredients
- 1 pound of salmon filets, cut into 1-inch cubes
- 1 cup of cherry tomatoes
- 1 cup of cubed zucchini
- 1 cup of cubed yellow squash
- 1 cup of cubed bell pepper
- 2 tablespoons of olive oil
- 1 tablespoon of chopped fresh herbs
- Salt and pepper to taste

Directions

Start by preheating your oven to 400 degrees Fahrenheit and greasing a baking sheet. The salmon cubes, cherry tomatoes, zucchini, yellow squash, and bell pepper should be threaded onto skewers in a manner that allows you to experiment with different combinations of foods. After the baking sheet has been prepped, place the skewers on it. In a small bowl, combine the olive oil, herbs, salt, and pepper by whisking those ingredients together. Apply the herb mixture to the skewers using a brush, making sure to coat them evenly. Place the skewers in an oven that has been warmed and roast them for fifteen to twenty minutes, or until the salmon is fully cooked and the vegetables are somewhat soft. Serve the skewers while they are still hot, and if preferred, garnish them with more herbs.

Chicken and brown rice bowl

In order to prepare a bowl of chicken and brown rice for individuals who have type 2 diabetes, you will require the following assortment of ingredients:

Ingredients
- 1 cup of uncooked brown rice
- 2 cups of water
- 1 tablespoon of olive oil
- 1 pound of boneless, skinless chicken breasts, cut into 1-inch cubes
- 1 cup of chopped vegetables
- ¼ cup of low-sodium chicken broth
- 2 cloves of garlic, minced
- 1 teaspoon of dried thyme

Directions

The brown rice should be cooked in accordance with the directions provided on the package, with water serving as the cooking liquid. As soon as the rice is done cooking, fluff it with a fork and then set it aside. Bring the olive oil to a simmer in a large skillet located over a medium heat. To the pan, add the chicken cubes and cook them for five to six minutes, or until they are completely cooked through. Put the chopped veggies, chicken stock, garlic, and thyme into the skillet and stir to combine. Cook the vegetables for a further five to six minutes, or until they reach the desired tenderness. To serve, divide the cooked brown rice among the bowls that will be used for serving, and then place the chicken and vegetable mixture on top of the rice. Eat your bowl of chicken and brown rice while it is still hot.

Supreme Diabetes Diet Cookbook

Turkey and cheese pinwheels

In order to craft pinwheels filled with turkey and cheese for individuals who suffer from type 2 diabetes, you will require the following ingredients:

Ingredients
- 8 whole wheat tortillas
- 8 ounces of sliced turkey breast
- 4 ounces of low-fat cream cheese, softened
- ½ cup of chopped fresh spinach
- ¼ cup of chopped sun-dried tomatoes
- ¼ cup of chopped red onion
- ¼ cup of chopped black olives
- Salt and pepper to taste

Directions

To begin, arrange the tortillas in a single layer on a flat, clean surface. The cream cheese should be spread in a thin layer over each tortilla, leaving a little border around the sides of the tortilla. After that, spread the sliced turkey, spinach, sun-dried tomatoes, red onion, and black olives across the tortillas in an even manner. Add salt and pepper to taste, and sprinkle with salt. Step three: Beginning at one end, carefully roll each tortilla into a cylinder that is as tight as possible. Make sure that each tortilla roll is covered in plastic wrap and placed in the refrigerator for at least half an hour so that the flavors may combine. When you are ready to serve, remove the tortilla rolls from their packaging and cut them into pinwheels measuring one inch in diameter. Either serve the pinwheels at room temperature or in a cooled state.

Black bean and corn salad

It is necessary to have the following items in order to make a salad consisting of black beans and corn for individuals who have type 2 diabetes:

Ingredients
- 1 can of black beans, drained and rinsed
- 1 cup of frozen corn, thawed
- ½ cup of diced red pepper
- ½ cup of diced red onion
- ¼ cup of chopped fresh cilantro
- 2 tablespoons of lime juice
- 1 tablespoon of olive oil
- ¼ teaspoon of cumin
- Salt and pepper

Directions

The black beans, which have been drained and washed, the corn that has been frozen, the diced red pepper, the diced red onion, and the chopped cilantro should be combined in a big bowl. In a small bowl, combine the lime juice, olive oil, cumin, and a bit of salt and pepper by whisking all of the ingredients together. Third, pour the dressing over the mixture of black beans and corn, and swirl it to blend the ingredients. You may either serve the black bean and corn salad right away or put it in the refrigerator until you are ready to eat it.

Chicken and avocado salad

It is necessary to have the following items in order to make a salad consisting of chicken and avocado for individuals who have type 2 diabetes:

Ingredients
- 2 cups of cooked and shredded chicken
- 1 avocado, diced
- ½ cup of cherry tomatoes, halved
- ¼ cup of diced red onion
- ¼ cup of chopped fresh cilantro
- 2 tablespoons of lime juice

- 1 tablespoon of olive oil
- Salt and pepper

Directions

Combine the shredded chicken, diced avocado, cherry tomatoes, diced red onion, and chopped cilantro in a large bowl. Mix until everything is evenly distributed. Place the lime juice, olive oil, and a bit of salt and pepper in a small bowl and whisk them together until they are combined. After pouring the dressing over the chicken and avocado mixture, toss with a spoon to incorporate the ingredients. You can either serve the chicken and avocado salad right away or put it in the refrigerator until you are ready to eat it.

Greek yogurt and fruit parfait

You will need the following materials in order to make a parfait consisting of Greek yogurt and fruit for children and adults who have type 2 diabetes:

Ingredients
- 1 cup of plain Greek yogurt
- ½ cup of fresh berries

- ¼ cup of chopped nuts, such as almonds, walnuts, or pecans
- 1 tablespoon of honey or maple syrup

Directions

Greek yogurt, fresh berries, and chopped almonds should be layered in a container such as a jar or cup. The second step is to drizzle honey or maple syrup over the fruit and almonds that are already on top. In the event that additional parfaits are desired, repeat the process of layering the ingredients. Immediately serve the parfaits made with Greek yogurt and fruit, or store them in the refrigerator until you are ready to consume them.

Roasted vegetable and quinoa bowls

In order to make a dish of quinoa and roasted vegetables for those who have type 2 diabetes, you will need the following ingredients:

Ingredients
- 1 cup of uncooked quinoa
- ½ cup of cherry tomatoes
- ½ cup of sliced zucchini
- ½ cup of sliced bell peppers
- ¼ cup of diced red onion
- 2 tablespoons of olive oil
- Salt and pepper
- ¼ cup of crumbled feta cheese

Directions
To prepare a baking sheet, line it with parchment paper and preheat the oven to 375 degrees Fahrenheit. Prepare the quinoa in accordance with the directions provided on the box. Place the cherry tomatoes, zucchini, bell peppers, and red onion in a bowl and add the olive oil that has been seasoned with salt and pepper. Toss the ingredients together. Arrange the veggies in a single layer on the baking sheet that has been prepared, and roast them in the oven for twenty to twenty-five minutes, or until

they are soft and have a little caramelization. To put together the bowl, start by placing a portion of cooked quinoa in the bottom of the bowl. Next, add the roasted veggies and crumbled feta cheese.

Supreme Diabetes Diet Cookbook

LUNCHTIME RECIPES

Supreme Diabetes Diet Cookbook

Breakfast quesadilla

Ingredients

- 1 whole wheat tortilla
- 1/4 cup shredded cheese
- 2 tablespoons chopped cooked bacon or sausage
- 1/4 cup cooked and crumbled tofu (optional)
- 1/4 cup chopped bell peppers
- 1/4 cup chopped onion
- 1/4 cup chopped tomato
- 1/4 cup chopped spinach
- Salt and pepper to taste

Directions

A skillet should be heated over medium heat. Place the tortilla in the skillet, and then spread the cheese over half of the tortilla in a uniform layer. Place the cheese on the tortilla, and then add the bacon or sausage, tofu (if you are using it), bell peppers, onion, tomato, and spinach around the cheese. Salt and pepper should be added to taste at this point. The fifth step is to carefully fold the tortilla over so that it forms a half-moon shape, and then softly press the edges to seal them. Cook the quesadilla for two to three minutes on each side, or until the cheese has melted and the tortilla has a light brown color. Immediately serve the quesadilla after cutting it into wedges and serving it.

Note:

The recipe for this morning dish is not only delicious but also satiating, and it is loaded with both protein and fiber. Additionally, it contains a minimal amount of carbohydrates, which makes it an excellent choice for individuals who have type 2 diabetes. To tailor the dish to your preferences, you can alter the ingredients by substituting different kinds of vegetables, meats, or cheeses.

Egg and cheese muffins

Ingredients

- 4 eggs
- ¼ cup milk ½ cup shredded cheese
- 1 cup diced vegetables
- Salt and pepper, to taste

Directions

Place paper liners inside a muffin tin and preheat the oven to 375 degrees Fahrenheit. Place the eggs and milk in a bowl and mix them together until they are thoroughly blended. Mix the shredded cheese and diced vegetables together in a mixing bowl. Distribute the egg mixture all over the muffin cups in an equitable manner, filling each one approximately three-quarters of the way. Add salt

Supreme Diabetes Diet Cookbook

and pepper to taste, and make sure you season the muffins. Place the muffins in the oven and bake for fifteen to twenty minutes, or until the eggs have finished setting and the muffins have a golden brown color. After removing the muffins from the oven, wait a few minutes before serving them so that they can cool down.

Note:

In addition, for an additional layer of flavor, you can incorporate a spoonful of chopped herbs or a sprinkle of diced ham into the muffin mixture. Make the necessary adjustments to the quantity and kind of components to meet your specific requirements and tastes.

Supreme Diabetes Diet Cookbook

Lunchtime Sandwich

Ingredients

- 1 slice turkey bacon
- 1 egg, fried or scrambled
- 1 slice whole grain bread
- 1/2 tomato, sliced
- 1/2 avocado, sliced
- Salt and pepper, to taste

Directions

To ensure that your turkey bacon is crispy and golden brown, cook it in a pan over medium heat until it reaches the desired outcome. Place the egg in the pan and continue to cook it until it reaches the amount of level of doneness that you choose. Add the slice of bread to the toaster and toast it until it is golden brown and crispy. After the bacon and egg have been cooked, place them on the toast, and then add the cut tomato and avocado. This is the fourth step in assembling the sandwich. Savor the sandwich by seasoning it with salt and pepper to your liking. Sixth, serve the sandwich as soon as possible, garnishing it with additional toppings of your choosing, such as lettuce, sliced red onion, or a dollop of mustard or mayonnaise.

Note:

A slice of cheese or a spoonful of hummus can also be added to the sandwich in order to increase the amount of protein and flavor it contains. Make the necessary adjustments to the quantity and kind of components to meet your specific requirements and tastes.

Grilled chicken salad

Ingredients

- 2 chicken breasts
- Salt and pepper
- 1 bag of mixed greens
- 1 avocado, diced
- 1 pint of cherry tomatoes, halved
- 1/4 cup of chopped walnuts or pecans
- 2 tablespoons of olive oil
- 1 tablespoon of red wine vinegar
- 1 teaspoon of Dijon mustard

Directions

Bring the temperature of your grill up to medium-high. The chicken breasts should be seasoned with salt, pepper, and any other herbs or spices that you consider to be appropriate. Place the chicken breasts on the grill and cook them for approximately six to eight minutes on each side, or until the internal temperature reaches 165 degrees Fahrenheit. While the chicken is cooking on the barbecue, you may make the salad by combining the bag of mixed greens, the diced avocado, the cherry tomatoes, and the chopped almonds. After the chicken has been cooked, allow it to reach room temperature for a few minutes before slicing it into strips. To prepare the dressing, combine the olive oil, red wine vinegar, and Dijon mustard in a bowl and mix them together. Assemble the salad by first laying the mixed greens on a dish, then adding the avocado, cherry tomatoes, and chopped nuts in accordance with the order listed above. Place the cut chicken on top, and then sprinkle the dressing over the chicken. 8. Serve the chicken salad that has been grilled almost immediately, and enjoy it.

Note:
The grilled chicken salad that you create with this recipe yields two servings. Because it is a meal that is not only delectable but also satiating, and because it contains protein, healthy fats, and complex carbohydrates, it is an excellent choice for individuals who have type 2 diabetes. It is the avocado and the nuts that contribute the beneficial fats, while the cherry tomatoes and the mixed

greens contribute the fiber and the nutrients. The dressing imparts flavor without contributing an excessive amount of additional calories or sugar. It is simple to modify this salad so that it incorporates the foods that you enjoy the most, and it may be served with a side of whole wheat bread, a small amount of quinoa, or brown rice.

Lunch burrito

Ingredients

- whole grain tortilla
- 4 eggs scrambled
- 1/2 cup black beans
- 1/4 cup salsa
- 1/4 cup shredded cheese
- Salt and pepper, to taste

Directions

Prepare the eggs by scrambling them in a pan over medium heat until they are completely cooked through. In a bowl, combine the scrambled eggs with the black beans, salsa, and shredded cheese. Stir until everything is incorporated. Salt and pepper should be added to the egg and bean combination according to personal preference. Arrange the tortilla on a dish, and then ladle the mixture of the egg and beans down the middle of the tortilla. Over the filling, fold the sides of the tortilla on top of each other. After that, fold it up tightly so that the filling is completely encased. Sixth, serve the tortilla as soon as possible, garnishing it with additional toppings of your choosing, such as chopped cilantro, sliced tomatoes, or a dollop of sour cream.

Note:

In order to increase the amount of nutrients that are present in the scrambled eggs, you may also include a handful of chopped veggies, such as bell peppers or onions. To accommodate your specific requirements and tastes, you can modify both the quantity and the kind of ingredients.

Salmon with quinoa and steamed broccoli

Ingredients
- 2 salmon filets
- 1 cup of quinoa
- 1 head of broccoli
- Olive oil
- Herbs and spices of your choice

Directions
To prepare the quinoa, follow the instructions on the box. Broccoli should be steamed until it is tender, after which it should be cut into little florets.

In step three, select the herbs and spices that you intend to use in order to season the salmon filets. A pan has been heated over medium heat, and a small amount of olive oil has been cooked in it. The salmon filets should be fully cooked after three to four minutes on each side of the cooking process. Present the salmon filets on plates, with the quinoa served on the side and the broccoli that has been steamed on top.

Note:

For those who suffer from type 2 diabetes, this dish offers an alternative that is both nutritious and satiating. In addition to providing protein and healthy fats, the salmon also contributes complex carbs and fiber, while the quinoa and broccoli contribute both. Herbs and spices impart taste without contributing any more calories or sugar to the dish. If you want to make the dish more interesting, you may experiment with different herbs and spices, and you can also adapt the recipe to suit your preferences and the requirements of your diet.

Supreme Diabetes Diet Cookbook

DINNER RECIPES

Turkey chili

Ingredients
- 1 pound of ground turkey
- 1 onion, diced
- 1 bell pepper, diced
- 1 can of diced tomatoes
- 1 can of black beans
- 1 cup of chicken broth
- Chili spices (such as cumin, paprika, and oregano)
- 1 avocado, diced
- ½ cup of cornbread mix

Directions

Place the ground turkey in a large pot and bring it to a simmer over medium heat. Prepare the turkey until it is browned and cooked all the way through. Put the diced tomatoes, diced onion, diced bell pepper, diced black beans, and chicken broth into the pot or saucepan. Before bringing the liquid to a boil, stir in the chili spices and stir them in. Once the vegetables have reached the desired level of doneness and the flavors have merged together, lower the heat to a low setting and continue to simmer the chili for twenty to thirty minutes. Place the chili in bowls, and serve it with a tiny portion of cornbread on the side. Top each bowl with a piece of diced avocado slice.

Note:

Individuals who have type 2 diabetes can benefit from this turkey chili because it is a healthy and tasty alternative. Protein is provided by the ground turkey, while fiber and complex carbs are provided by the veggies and black beans contained in the dish. The dish is enhanced with a creamy and slightly sweet flavor thanks to the addition of cornbread and avocado. If you want to make the dish more interesting, you may experiment with different herbs and spices, and you can also adapt the recipe to suit your preferences and the requirements of your diet.

Shrimp and zucchini noodles

Ingredients

- 1 pound of shrimp
- 2 zucchini
- 1 cup of broccoli florets
- Olive oil
- Garlic, minced
- Herbs and spices of your choice

Directions

Through the process of spiralizing the zucchini, you may make noodles out of the veggie. A pan has been heated over medium heat, and a small amount of olive oil has been cooked in it. Add the minced garlic and wait approximately two minutes, or until the aroma is released. Adding the shrimp to

the pan and sautéing them for two to three minutes on each side at the point when they are pink and cooked through is the third step. When the broccoli florets have reached the softer stage, add them to the pan and continue to simmer for an additional three minutes. After two to three minutes of cooking, zucchini noodles are added and simmered until they are completely cooked.
Place the shrimp and zucchini noodles in bowls and sprinkle the top with the herbs and spices of your choice prior to serving.

Note:
For those who suffer from diabetes, this dish offers an alternative that is both nutritious and satiating. Protein is provided by the shrimp, while complex carbohydrates and fiber are provided by the broccoli and other vegetables, including the zucchini noodles. The spices and herbs contribute taste without adding any additional calories or sugar to the dish. If you want to make the dish more interesting, you may experiment with different herbs and spices, and you can also adapt the recipe to suit your preferences and the requirements of your diet.

Baked chicken and sweet potato

Ingredients

- 2 chicken breasts
- 1 sweet potato, diced
- 1 cup of spinach
- Olive oil
- Herbs and spices of your choice

Directions

Put your oven on to a temperature of 400 degrees Fahrenheit. Season the chicken breasts with the herbs and spices of your choosing from the list provided. Place the chicken and sweet potato in a baking dish and mix them together. Pour a small amount of olive oil over the top. The sweet potato should be cooked through and the chicken should be cooked through after 20 to 25 minutes in the oven. In the meantime, wilt the spinach by steaming it until it is tender. Place the steamed spinach on the side and serve the cooked chicken and sweet potato alongside it

Note:

For those who suffer from diabetes, this dish offers an alternative that is both nutritious and satiating. Protein is provided by the chicken, while complex carbohydrates and fiber are provided by the sweet potato and spinach. The spices and herbs contribute taste without adding any additional calories or sugar to the dish. If you want to make the dish more interesting, you may experiment with different herbs and spices, and you can also adapt the recipe to suit your preferences and the requirements of your diet.

Eggplant Parmesan

Ingredients

- 1 eggplant, sliced into ¼ inch rounds
- 1 egg, beaten
- 1 cup of breadcrumbs
- ½ cup of grated Parmesan cheese
- 1 cup of marinara sauce
- 1 cup of steamed spinach

Directions

Put your oven on to a temperature of 400 degrees Fahrenheit. Coat the eggplant slices with breadcrumbs and grated Parmesan cheese after dipping them in the egg that has been beaten well. Put the eggplant slices that have been coated on a baking sheet and bake them for fifteen to twenty minutes, or until they have a golden brown color and are soft. In the meantime, wilt the spinach by steaming it until it is tender. In order to put together the Eggplant Parmesan, start by spreading a layer of marinara sauce that covers the bottom of a baking dish. First, a layer of eggplant slices should be placed on top, and then another layer of marinara sauce should be added. The layers should be repeated until all of the eggplant slices have been utilized. 6. Add some additional grated Parmesan cheese to the top of the dish and evenly distribute it. Continue baking the Eggplant Parmesan for an additional fifteen to twenty minutes, or until the cheese becomes a bubbly and melted consistency.Serve the Eggplant Parmesan with a side of steamed spinach.

Note:
An alternative that is both delicious and satiating for people who have type 2 diabetes is this Eggplant Parmesan pasta dish. Additionally, the spinach contributes additional nutrients, while the eggplant is a source of fiber. Cheese is a flavor enhancer that does not provide an excessive amount of additional calories or carbohydrates. If you want to make the dish more interesting, you may experiment with different herbs and spices, and you can also adapt the recipe to suit your preferences and the requirements of your diet.

Supreme Diabetes Diet Cookbook

Supreme Diabetes Diet Cookbook

Black bean and quinoa salad

Ingredients
- 1 cup of cooked quinoa
- 1 can of black beans, rinsed and drained
- 1 cup of cherry tomatoes, halved
- 1 avocado, diced
- ¼ cup of chopped cilantro
- 1 lime, juiced
- 1 tablespoon of olive oil
- Herbs and spices of your choice

Directions
Combine the quinoa that has been cooked, the black beans, the cherry tomatoes, the avocado, and the cilantro in a large bowl. Place the lime juice, olive oil, and various herbs and spices in a small basin and whisk those ingredients together. After

pouring the dressing over the quinoa mixture, toss it to blend the ingredients. To serve, place the salad in dishes and, if wanted, garnish it with more herbs and spices.

Note:

For those who suffer from type 2 diabetes, this salad made with quinoa and black beans is a choice that is both nutritious and delectable. It is the avocado that contributes the good fats, while the quinoa and black beans are the sources of protein and fiber. Herbs and spices impart taste without contributing any more calories or sugar to the dish. If you want to make the dish more interesting, you may experiment with different herbs and spices, and you can also adapt the recipe to suit your preferences and the requirements of your diet.

Beef and broccoli stir-fry

Ingredients

- 1 pound of beef sirloin, sliced into thin strips
- 1 head of broccoli, cut into small florets
- 1 bell pepper, sliced
- 1 onion, sliced
- 1 cup of snow peas
- 2 cloves of garlic, minced
- 1 tablespoon of ginger, grated
- ¼ cup of low-sodium soy sauce
- 1 cup of cooked brown rice

Directions

A large pan or wok should be heated over high heat. After adding the meat, stir-fry it for two to three minutes, or until it is completely cooked through. Increase the heat to high and stir-fry the broccoli, bell pepper, onion, and snow peas for an additional two to three minutes, or until the veggies have reached the desired level of tenderness. The next step is to combine the minced garlic, grated ginger, and low-sodium soy sauce in a small bowl and whisk them together. After stirring the sauce into the pan, continue to stir-fry the ingredients for one to two minutes, or until the sauce has reached the desired temperature. Place the stir-fry on top of a bed of brown rice that has been prepared.

Note:
An alternative that is both nutritious and satiating for people who have type 2 diabetes is this stir-fry dish that features beef and vegetables. The meat is a source of protein, while the vegetables are a source of fiber and complex carbs. A flavorful addition that does not add an excessive amount of additional calories or carbohydrates is the sauce. If you want to make the dish more interesting, you may experiment with different herbs and spices, and you can also adapt the recipe to suit your preferences and the requirements of your diet.

Vegetable and bean soup

Ingredients

- 1 tablespoon of olive oil
- 1 onion, diced
- 2 carrots, peeled and diced
- 2 celery stalks, diced
- 1 can of diced tomatoes
- 1 can of kidney beans, rinsed and drained
- 1 cup of vegetable broth
- Herbs and spices of your choice
- ½ cup of whole grain bread

Directions

Warm the olive oil in a large saucepan by heating it over a medium flame. Put in the carrots, celery, and onion, and continue to boil for another five to six minutes, or until the veggies are soft. Put the kidney beans, diced tomatoes, vegetable broth, herbs, and spices into the saucepan. Add the remaining ingredients. After the mixture has reached a boil, turn the heat down to a low setting and allow the soup to simmer for twenty to thirty minutes, or until the veggies have reached the desired level of tenderness and the flavors have merged together. The soup should be served in bowls, and a small portion of whole grain bread should be placed on the side table.

Note:
People who have type 2 diabetes can benefit from this vegetable and bean soup, which is both nutritious and satiating when consumed. A source of fiber is provided by the vegetables, while the beans provide a source of protein and complex carbs. Herbs and spices impart taste without contributing any more calories or sugar to the dish. If you want to make the dish more interesting, you may experiment with different herbs and spices, and you can also adapt the recipe to suit your preferences and the requirements of your diet.

Grilled turkey and vegetable skewers

Ingredients

- 1 pound of turkey breast, cut into 1-inch pieces
- 1 bell pepper, cut into 1-inch pieces
- 1 onion, cut into 1-inch pieces
- 1 cup of cherry tomatoes
- 1 cup of your choice of vegetables
- 1 cup of cooked quinoa or brown rice
- Olive oil

Directions

Bring the temperature of your grill up to medium-high. Thread the turkey, bell pepper, onion, cherry tomatoes, and any other vegetables of your choosing onto skewers. Place the skewers on the grill and cook them for six to eight minutes on each side, or until the turkey is fully cooked and the vegetables are soft and have a slight scorched flavor. Arrange the skewers in a single layer on top of a bed of quinoa or brown rice, and if preferred, drizzle them with a little olive oil and season them with additional herbs and spices.

Note:

For those who suffer from diabetes, this dish offers an alternative that is both nutritious and satiating. Protein is provided by the turkey, while complex carbohydrates and fiber are provided by the vegetables and either quinoa or brown rice depending on the dish. Herbs and spices impart taste without contributing any more calories or sugar to the dish. If you want to make the dish more interesting, you may experiment with different herbs and spices, and you can also adapt the recipe to suit your preferences and the requirements of your diet.

Frozen Yogurt Bark

Ingredients

- 1 cup of plain Greek yogurt
- ¼ cup of sugar-free maple syrup
- 1 teaspoons of vanilla extract
- Unsweetened coconut
- Chopped nuts
- Sugar-free dried fruit

Directions

Prepare the mixture by combining one cup of plain Greek yogurt, one-fourth cup of sugar-free maple syrup, and one teaspoon of vanilla extract in a mixing dish of medium size. Combine thoroughly until the mixture is smooth. Put the yogurt mixture on a baking sheet that has been lined with parchment paper and spread it out evenly. Check to see that the yogurt is distributed evenly and has a thickness of approximately half an inch. Sprinkle the yogurt with the toppings of your choice of toppings. Unsweetened coconut, chopped nuts (like almonds or walnuts), and sugar-free dried fruit (like cranberries or cherries) are some of the options that are beneficial for individuals who have type 2 diabetes. Put the baking sheet in the freezer and freeze it for at least two hours, or until the yogurt has reached a solid state due to the freezing process. When the yogurt has reached the frozen state, divide it into little pieces or break it up into chunks by using a knife that is sharp. As a nutritious snack throughout the day, keep your frozen yogurt bark on hand for consumption. You have the ability to keep it in the freezer for up to a week if you put it in an airtight container.

Note:
To accommodate your individual preferences and tastes, this recipe can be readily modified to suit your needs. There are a variety of varieties of yogurt that you may experiment with, such as strawberry or vanilla, as well as a variety of toppings, such as chocolate chips or chopped dark chocolate. If you want to keep the frozen yogurt bark suitable for people who have type 2 diabetes,

you should make sure to use components that are low in sugar and high in protein.

CONCLUSION

It's evident by the end of the "Supreme Diabetes Diet Cookbook: Delicious and Easy to Cook Healthy Recipes for Every Home" that flavor and the love of cooking don't have to be sacrificed in order to manage diabetes. As this book has demonstrated, a rich, varied, and incredibly fulfilling diet is still possible for those with diabetes. Every recipe has been thoughtfully created to support healthy blood sugar regulation while providing your body with nourishment. These recipes are made to easily fit into your lifestyle, whether you're cooking a short weeknight supper or something special for your loved ones. This makes eating healthy both doable and pleasurable. Recall that controlling diabetes is a journey, one that is facilitated by having the appropriate resources and an optimistic outlook. Making healthy food choices and paying attention to portion proportions are significant steps in the right direction. More than that, though, you're adopting a diet that honors flavor, vitality, and the joy of sharing delicious food with others. I hope that as you work through these recipes, you'll be motivated not only by the food, but also by the realization that you're actively managing your own health. This cookbook will prove that, with the correct mindset, every meal can be a step toward a healthier, happier you. Let it be your guide as you learn to live well with diabetes. I am grateful that you let me share in your adventure. I hope you enjoy many more delectable and healthful dinners with the people you care about.

Printed in Great Britain
by Amazon